By

Eric Christopher Hoelle

BLACK BOX THEATRE PUBLISHING

Copyright© 2013 by Eric Hoelle
ALL RIGHTS RESERVED
CAUTION: Professionals and amateurs are hereby warned that
Infectious
is subject to a royalty. It is fully protected under the copyright laws
of the United States of America, the British Commonwealth,
including Canada, and all other countries of the Copyright Union.

All rights, including professional, amateur, motion
picture, recitation, lecturing, public reading, radio broadcasting,
television and the rights of translation into foreign languages
are strictly reserved. The right to photocopy scripts or videotape
performances can be granted only by the author. In some cases,
the author may choose to allow this, provided permission has
been requested prior to the production. No alterations, deletions
or substitutions may be made to the work without the
written permission of the author.

All publicity material must contain the author's name,
as the sole author of the work. By producing this play you give the
author and BLACK BOX THEATRE PUBLISHING
the right to use any publicity material including pictures, programs
and posters generated from the production.

To order additional copies of the script, or
to request performance rights, please contact us at
wwwblackboxtheatrepublishing.com

ISBN 978-0615829104

Printed in the United States of America.

CAST

Vivian
The Son
James
Steve
The Woman

INFECTIOUS
ACT ONE SCENE ONE

AT RISE: A young black WOMAN steps outside HER little
house. The house is in a remote section of rural
1960's era Mississippi. As SHE yawns and looks
out into the sky, SHE closes HER eyes for a
second and smiles. As SHE opens HER eyes SHE
is brought back into reality. HER face turns into
one of misery again. SHE steps off her porch
heading down stage right towards a tombstone
that's on HER land.

VIVIAN
Here I go now.
>(SHE takes a deep breath.)

It's me again your... Your...
>(Struggling.)

Your wife... It's about going on eight months now since they killed... since you were taken from here from here by god. By god... I still don't know how to feel about what happened. Why did I say that?
>(SHE starts to lose it but SHE holds HER tears back.)

Why could I never say to you how I felt in life but now in death I still stop myself on what I needed to say to you in life...
>(Deep breathe.)

I do miss you ...
>(Pause)

um I do miss you in ways. We have a son, your son. I had your son. I don't know how to raise him like you did. He's changed so much since you were gone.
>(Annoyed.)

He looks like you. I wish I knew what to do. A mother should know how to handle her son. Right? He still is mine too even know what you did to...

                    SON
Mom!

                    VIVIAN
          (Startled SHE quickly puts HER hands over HER
          mouth.)
You're going to school now?

                    SON
I'm going.

                    VIVIAN
Now?

                    SON
Yeah.

                    VIVIAN
Say yes.

                    SON
Yeah, yes what's the difference.

                    VIVIAN
Better you represent yourself. The better you will be received.

                    SON
Ok… I'm going.

                    VIVIAN
Goodbye.

                    SON
Bye.

                    VIVIAN
Would you um? Make sure you don't talk to anyone you
don't know to and from-

                    SON
Yeah, I mean yes I know. I know.

                    VIVIAN
There. And make sure you take the same way home-

                    SON
            (Interrupts.)
Yeah. Bye.
            (HE exits.)

                    VIVIAN
Yes bye. I... I love
            (SHE starts to lose it again.)
I
            (To HERSELF.)
I love you. Yes.
            (Deep breathe.)
I hope.
            (Turns to the grave.)
Time to go on with the rest of my day.

                        VIVIAN walks to the steps and up onto the
                        porch there is pile of laundry in a basket
                        sitting on the porch, SHE picks it up comes
                        down the steps and over to where the line
                        hangs and starts to place the laundry on the
                        line. SOUND: Birds chirping and buzzards.
                        A black MAN approaches as SHE starts to
                        hang the clothes. HE watches HER for a
                        second. HE clearly has a deep attraction for
                        HER. SHE turns around and is startled for a
                        second before realizing whom it is.

                    VIVIAN
Oh!
            (Dropping the rest of the clothes.)

JAMES
Excuse me Miss Vivian I didn't mean to startle you. I just was passing by.

VIVIAN
Oh, Mr. Chaney.
> (SHE starts to pick up the clothes.)

Oh, sorry. It's quite all right. I just didn't...
> (HE walks over to help HER with the clothes)

No, please don't trouble yourself I have them.

JAMES
You sure Miss Vivian?

VIVIAN
"Mrs." I just didn't see you there, you startled me.
> (SHE picks up all the clothes in the basket and stands up.)

JAMES

Pardon?

VIVIAN
I said I didn't see you there. You startled me.

JAMES
No, before that when I said Miss Vivian.

VIVIAN
Oh I see, I said "Mrs.", when you said, "Miss."

JAMES
(Disappointed.)
Oh yes, of course.

VIVIAN
After all I'm still a married woman, of course.

JAMES
Pardon me about that too Miss, I mean Mrs. Vivian.

VIVIAN
It's really alright, Mr. Chaney.

JAMES
Thank you again Mrs. Vivian.

VIVIAN
What can I help you with Mr. Chaney?

JAMES
Just passing by wanted to say hi and see how you're all doing.

VIVIAN
Oh thank you… I'm fine Mr. Chaney. Thank you.

JAMES
And your son, how's he?

VIVIAN
Really well… Thank you for asking.

JAMES
Can I offer you a cigarette Miss Vivian?

VIVIAN
No thank you I don't smoke.

JAMES
I only do sometimes, once in a while.

VIVIAN
Well please do not on my account, I just never took to it.

JAMES
They say it may cause some kind of throat problems I believe they say. I forgot who told me that, one of the whites in town. But...

VIVIAN
(Interrupting.)
All the more reason not to if that's what people are saying.

JAMES
I was smoking since nine no problems here.

VIVIAN
Well yes. I do need to get on with my day anything else I can do for you Mr. Chaney?

JAMES
I'm heading over to the store can I pick you up anything?

VIVIAN
I believe I don't need anything, but thanks for asking.

JAMES
Maybe if, I don't know... Would you like if I picked up some food, you could cook it and we could have it tonight.

VIVIAN
Oh um...

JAMES
If you are free that is Miss Vivian?

VIVIAN
Um you do remember it was not too long ago that.

JAMES
Oh say no more. I thought it would just be nice to have a meal with someone.

VIVIAN
My son, I have a son here to.

JAMES
Oh… Yes… he can join us to that food it's not a problem. I can pick up some extra.

VIVIAN
Tonight I do not think is good.

JAMES
Tomorrow?

VIVIAN
Please stop by the next after tomorrow. See how I feel. I'm sorry Mr. Chaney I'm not feeling good, I mean well, today.

JAMES
Yes of course Miss Vivian. Have a good day and please if you need anything.

VIVIAN
Thank you Mr. Chaney.

> MR. CHANEY exits. VIVIAN stands there with a forced smile on HER face. SHE turns and looks back at the grave.

VIVIAN
I will only be able to fight them off for so long. It's already starting again. A polite interaction, I know nothing else but you. Why did you have to do what you did and then why did you have to go and leave me here broken with no way to heal. It's exhausting talking like this. I am broken all around. I need a guardian again.
    (SHE'S about to cry.)

STEVE
(Offstage.)
Excuse me?

VIVIAN
(SHE looks up.)
Huh?

STEVE
(Offstage.)
Hello? Excuse me?

VIVIAN
(Fear gives way in HER face. SHE jumps up.)
What can I do for you sir?

STEVE
(Offstage.)
Excuse me I didn't mean to startle you while you were talking yourself. But I think I'm lost. Trying to get back to Meridian. You think you can help me?

VIVIAN
Yes sir.

STEVE enters.

STEVE
Thank you miss, I really did not mean to intrude.
It's so hot today and I'm already so lost. I have a map here.
(HE pulls out a map.)
If you can point out how to get back, that would be great I get confused when it comes to verbal directions.

                    VIVIAN
I'm sorry...
          (SHE looks at HIM. HE looks at HER.)
I'm sorry what can I do for... You're not from around here
are you?

                    STEVE
Is it that obvious? Oh wait, it's because I'm lost of course.
Yea if I'd been from here I wouldn't be asking for directions.

                    VIVIAN
If you were from here you would not be asking me for
directions.

                    STEVE
Why?

                    VIVIAN
Because...
          (SHE looks down at HERSELF.)
What is it that you're looking for?

                    STEVE
The main-

                    VIVIAN
The main road, right!

                    STEVE
Great.

                    VIVIAN
All you need to do is make a left at the end of this block
and...

                    STEVE
Please.... the map.

VIVIAN
Oh, right sorry.

STEVE
That's quite alright.

VIVIAN
I'm sorry you just have to. You just have to… Are you on foot?

STEVE
No, my car's parked down the road.

VIVIAN
You just have...
>   (SHE looks at the map again then looks back up and points.)

...you just have to make the left at the end of the block and you make a left I mean a… right at-

STEVE
Please just show me on the map.

VIVIAN
It's very easy.

STEVE
I'm sure it is but I am better by using the map.

VIVIAN
Well um.

STEVE
Can you not…
>   (SHE looks at HIM, embarrassed.)

Oh, sorry.

VIVIAN
It's ok.

STEVE
So sorry, I didn't mean to embarrass you.

VIVIAN
You're not the first man to embarrass me.

STEVE
Well, we aren't all bad, I hope….

VIVIAN
Just about every white man has been.

STEVE
Well I am not 'as bad', I hope.

VIVIAN
I really need to get back to-

STEVE
Your line just came down.

VIVIAN
What? Oh not again!
(VIVIAN walks over to the clothesline. HE follows HER.)

STEVE
Let me help.

VIVIAN
No, please don't trouble yourself.

STEVE
Really it's fine. I insist.
(HE starts to pick up the clothes with HER.)

                    VIVIAN
This is very kind, sir.

                    STEVE
Here's your bra...
          (SHE grabs it out of HIS hand.)
I tell you, even on these really hot days the wind doesn't do that much, huh?

                    VIVIAN
Some days, but when you lived here all your life it's just -

                    STEVE
          (Interrupts.)
Of the norm?

                    VIVIAN
Pardon?

                    STEVE
What?

                    VIVIAN
Of the norm?

                    STEVE
Yea normal. When you lived here every day of your life it just seems normal.

                    VIVIAN
That's right.

                    STEVE
But just because you lived here all your life and every man... every white man has been nasty to you doesn't mean that should just be normal.

VIVIAN
I really have to get back to-

STEVE
(Interrupts.)
Cigarette?
(Pulls out HIS cigarettes.)

VIVIAN
No thank you. Where are you from, if you don't mind me asking?

STEVE
New York.

VIVIAN
Are you with the civil rights? Because I do not want to be involved.

STEVE
No, I'm a photographer.

VIVIAN
Photographer?

STEVE
Yeah, I'm passing through, taking photos of whatever catches my eye, great images of beauty.

VIVIAN
Oh, you find any out here?

STEVE
Yea, I'm looking at one right now.
(Puts a cigarette in HIS mouth looks for HIS lighter but gets caught up in the conversation and forgets.)

                        VIVIAN
I really need to-

                        STEVE
Yea you really need to get back to what you were doing. I
know but hey look at the time! It's lunchtime I think.
Everyone can use a break. I have some cold beer in the back
at my car. Would you care for one?

                        VIVIAN
It's a little too early, don't you think, to be drinking?

                        STEVE
Not if the beer you were planning to have was from last night.
Then I think it's late on the drinking. I have some chicken
too.

                        VIVIAN
I...really, this is not a good idea.

                        STEVE
Why? You married?

                        VIVIAN
People may see.

                        STEVE
            (HE looks around.)
You seem to be pretty far out of the way.... Here. Look I
don't mean to impose I would love to take a few shots of you.
You have a beautiful face lovely skin. But, hey, if you need
to get back to what you were doing it's ok.

                        VIVIAN
            (Stunned.)
Can I have that cigarette please?

STEVE

Sure.
>(Hands HER a cigarette.)

Lighter is…
>(Starts to feel around.)

Lighter is… In the car
>(Takes the cigarette out of HIS mouth.)

I think… yea I'll be right back.

VIVIAN

It's fine then.

STEVE

I'm Steve. You're?

VIVIAN

Vivian.

STEVE

Vivian. Pretty name for a pretty girl, Vivian. It will just take me 5 minutes I'll go get my camera and the beer too, if you change your mind.

VIVIAN

Well then I guess I should clean up if you're going to take my picture then.

STEVE

No, don't! I like you just the way you are.
>(VIVIAN watches HIM walk away. SHE goes up to the porch and quickly washes HER face.)

VIVIAN

What am I doing? I'm a married woman. I was a married woman. Was…. was. Was! No. I can do this I can do this. I can he's just a guy he's just a guy. He's a white man. He's white. I can't do this. Just say sorry you can't do this, be polite.

(Steve walks back on stage)

STEVE

Hi.

VIVIAN

Hi. Oh good, the chicken. Let me take that from you put it on a plate.

STEVE

Ok. Thanks.

VIVIAN

Thank you, that's very nice of you… And I was not talking to myself.

STEVE

I'm not imposing, am I? Really I can go.

VIVIAN

My husband died two months ago.

STEVE

Wow! I'm sorry.

VIVIAN

You're the first person that I had to tell. Everybody else already knew. It's nice to be able to do it that way if you don't say it you can't admit it.

STEVE
Yeah, it's good to know, I guess that's the problem living in a small town. Everyone knows.

VIVIAN
Let me get some plates for the chicken. What's that?

STEVE
Oh it's a shirt, I'm covered in sweat. Is there a place I could wash up?

VIVIAN
Around back.

STEVE
Is it ok?

VIVIAN
Yes.

STEVE
You sure?

VIVIAN
No.

> VIVIAN steps up onto HER porch and fixes HER clothes facing upstage. SHE turns around to see HIS still looking at HER.)

STEVE
My condolences about your husband.
(Under HIS breath.)
Even though that's better for me.

> STEVE walks around back turns on the hose and rinses off. SHE comes out with two plates and sneaks a peak at HIM. Realizing

HER hair is up SHE quickly puts it down.
STEVE turns off the hose and walks back
over.

VIVIAN
Oh, let me get you a towel.

STEVE
Please, no need... it's hot... it's nice to be a little wet.

VIVIAN
I guess I'm just use to it.

STEVE
You never just get a little wet?

VIVIAN
Would you like some of this chicken?

STEVE
Yes please... Pardon the double entendre.
(SHE serves HIM chicken.)

VIVIAN
The what... Ok.
(SHE starts to eat the chicken nervously.)
It's good

STEVE
Thanks for joining me. I have not been able to eat with a single soul. I've been on the road so much.

VIVIAN
This is the first time... I ever had.... Never mind.

STEVE
First time for what?

VIVIAN
First time, I'm eating with a white man.

STEVE
How's it going so far?

VIVIAN
Are you ok?

STEVE
I think so. Why?

VIVIAN
I don't think um... Who are you?

STEVE
Steve again. Vivian. Pretty name.

VIVIAN
I don't think I ever heard anyone talk like you before.

STEVE
I'm not crazy if that what you're asking Vivian. Just a little....

VIVIAN
Do you call everyone that you don't know by their first name?

STEVE
Not if I don't know their first name... Man! You got some wall around you.
(HE stands up and pulls HIS camera out.)
Let see if we can break that wall down.

VIVIAN
Photos, now?

STEVE
If that's okay?

VIVIAN
What do I do?

STEVE
Just be you the real you.

HE takes a photo of HER

VIVIAN
Should I smile? I really don't know what to do.

STEVE
Sure! Knock yourself out.
(HE takes another shot.)
Let's see if we can get that laundry line in the background.
There we go.
(HE takes another shot.)

VIVIAN
I looked away.

STEVE
That's fine. Do whatever.
(Another shot.)

VIVIAN
Anything? How about if I put my head down?

STEVE
That's fine too.
(Another shot.)

VIVIAN
Arm over my head?

STEVE
That's fine too.
(Another shot.)

VIVIAN
Anything I can do that's not fine?

STEVE
Yeah...
(Another shot.)
You not being in them.
(VIVIAN laughs.)
Can I ask you a serious question?
(Another photo.)

VIVIAN
What?

STEVE
How did your husband die?

As SHE changes the look on HER face. HE shoots a bunch of shots.

VIVIAN
He was. He died, he... Is that beer still being offered?

HE stops photographing.

STEVE
Absolutely.

VIVIAN
May I?

STEVE
Of course, they are still surprisingly cold even in this heat.
>(HE takes two cans of beer out of HIS bag and opens them.)

Here.

VIVIAN
Thank you.

STEVE
What did you do with that cigarette?
>(Pulls out HIS lighter.)

VIVIAN
I think I...
>(Pause.)

I must of left it inside. I'll get it.

STEVE
No it's fine. Would you like another cig for now?

VIVIAN
Um, I'm fine thank you.

>HE lights HIS cigarette up.

STEVE
So how did if you don't mind me asking again, how did your husband pass away?

VIVIAN
Where are you from sir?

STEVE
Call me Steve. New York City.

VIVIAN

New York! Oh wow! You're really far from home. Now it makes sense.

STEVE

What does?

VIVIAN

You're a Yankee!

STEVE

I don't play baseball.

VIVIAN

I mean you're from the city.

STEVE

I know it's a joke.

VIVIAN

Now it makes sense. They always say the Yankees are a little weird, that explains it.

STEVE

I don't think of myself as weird.

VIVIAN

Oh you are. I mean no other white man would be photographing me and eating chicken with me unless they are a little weird.

                    STEVE
               (Annoyed.)
Well I don't see why it has to be that way. But it kind of
makes sense because the blacks back home always say the
blacks down south are a lot slower. Otherwise…
               (HER reaction changes. HE takes a photo of HER
               again.)
That's a good one.

                    VIVIAN
That's really.

                    STEVE
Hey you started and I can read by the way.

                    VIVIAN
I need to get back to….

                    STEVE
To the chores… Yeah I got it. So how the fuck do I get back
to Meridian?

                    VIVIAN
You can read, why don't you look at your map. And don't
forget your food.

               SHE goes to hand HIM the chicken, STEVE
               grabs VIVIAN and kisses HER. VIVIAN
               drops the food and HE lets HER pull away.

STEVE

That was…
>(SHE then kisses HIM as SHE does so SHE starts to pound at HIS chest in a violent manner. STEVE goes to put HER arms behind HER and SHE mumbles something in a hostile tone while kissing HIM. VIVIAN takes HIS hand and puts it between HER legs. SHE then pulls away. SHE is in shock. HE looks down and takes a piece of chicken from the plate on the ground and starts to eat it till there is nothing left but the bone. He drops the bone, takes a final drink of his beer and grabs HIS camera to leave.)

…not a bad piece of meat either.

VIVIAN

That's not funny.

STEVE

Neither is your reaction… I'm going to...

VIVIAN

Go!

STEVE

Go, yeah right.

> STEVE exits. VIVIAN starts to look at the sky SHE shrinks down towards the ground puts HER hand on HER forehead.

VIVIAN

My lord I am afraid of all my sufferings; I know that you will not hold me innocent.
>(SHE stops and looks around.)

It has gotten hot today.

> LIGHTS: Black out.

ACT ONE SCENE TWO

AT RISE: VIVIAN is sitting on the porch staring out into the sky. It is dark outside, HER SON approaches. SHE is holding the cigarettes that STEVE gave to HER but SHE is not smoking it. JAMES approaches. The SON goes in without saying a word.

JAMES
I found him Miss Vivian.

VIVIAN
Thank you, Mr. Chaney. I'm sorry to trouble you so late.

JAMES
It's really alright, happy to help.

VIVIAN
Where was...
(SHE corrects HERSELF.)
Where had he been?

JAMES
He was talking to that young girl down the road a ways.

VIVIAN
Was he?

JAMES
Was he what?

VIVIAN
You know sinning.

JAMES
Kissing? They were just kissing.

VIVIAN
You know how kissing leads to other… you know 'other things'…He's growing up too fast. He's twelve years old… that boy's too young to be growing up so fast. It's not right they don't know what they're doing at that age. I didn't. I didn't want to.

JAMES
Would you like a light for that cigarette Miss Vivian?

VIVIAN
What? Oh this… I found this.
>(SHE throws it off the porch onto the ground.)

JAMES
I really don't think he's too young Miss Vivian but I'll have a talk with him for you.

VIVIAN
Thank you Mr. Chaney but
>(Pause)

that won't be… What's the word? That won't be necessary.

JAMES
>(HE puts HIS hand on HER shoulders.)

I would really like to help with you and everything.
>(HE goes in for a hug but SHE pulls HER body away.)

VIVIAN
It's late Mr. Chaney, but thank you for your help.

JAMES
I understand… but I'd be pleased to come over again.

VIVIAN
Um… yes of course.

JAMES
Hope to next time… to spend some time.

VIVIAN
Have a good night and thank you.

JAMES
Good night Miss Vivian.

> JAMES, somewhat bewildered, shrugs and slowly turns to walk away. JAMES then exits.

VIVIAN
(VIVIAN prays looking at the tombstone.)
I don't want to go in there. I don't want to see him. I'm his mother. I'm his mother!
(SHE puts HER hand over HER head.)
What's wrong with me? It's not his fault… he was just he was just… born. It was yours the fathers.
(Deep breath. SHE holds in tears.)
Why did you do that to me? I live in my own hell.

> SHE walks away into the house. LIGHTS: The dark lights quickly become bright, as now it's daylight. SHE comes out of the house half asleep SHE fixes herself and walks over to the gravesite.

ACT ONE SCENE THREE

VIVIAN
Can't sleep again I don't know if it's because of what you did to me or because you're not beside me. Why couldn't you have gone away before you went away?

STEVE
(Offstage.)
Excuse me miss?
(VIVIAN, startled at first, recognizes the voice without turning around. SHE takes a deep breath as a nervous excitement takes over HER. STEVE enters carrying flowers)
Good morning... kind of... still.... somewhat.

VIVIAN
(A loss of words.)
Hi.... Um hello.

STEVE
It's the Yankee... Doodle. Dandy. Is it ok if I re-enter again? Your property, that is.

VIVIAN
You are already here. What's that?

STEVE
I believe they're called flowers.
(Laughs.)
A man I hope has given you flowers before? Otherwise there really is something wrong with all men in this town.

VIVIAN
Are you getting a kick out of this?

STEVE
Out of what?

VIVIAN

What, you come all away out here and say, 'Hey whites and the black don't mix, let me try to…. disturb that. Let me try to come here, all away from the big rich city and try to get some poor black girl. Let me try something new.' Do you know where you are? Do you know where this will lead? Bad things? That's where!

STEVE

Well, that's an interesting observation. Who's reading you that idea? That's exactly right that's how I get my fucking jolly's. Come all away out here to fuck "Colored girls" and then to drive all away back to "The Big Rich City" where I live in a tiny studio apartment and keep all my pennies.

VIVIAN

That's um…

STEVE

Sarcasm.

VIVIAN

Yes that's sarcasm.
    (Repeats it to HERSELF under HER breath.)
Sarcasm. Sarcasm.

STEVE

You're pretty tough. Only pretty tough but very pretty. These are for you...
    (HE holds the flowers up.)
…for your hospitality yesterday and I'm sorry for getting annoyed.

VIVIAN

And out of line.

STEVE

I'm not going to be sorry for that.

VIVIAN
Thank you, they're very nice.

STEVE
You've received flowers from a guy before, haven't you?
(SHE looks down.)
Dam shame.

VIVIAN
I have something inside, I think, to put them in.

STEVE
You are going to invite me in for the tour, if I'm not being too forward?

VIVIAN
It's against the law.

> SHE starts to walk up the steps holding the flowers.

STEVE
What? For a man to be in a woman's house?

VIVIAN
A white person.

STEVE
Seriously? Is that a state law?

VIVIAN
Yes and I would have said no anyway.
(SHE goes into the house and steps back out.)
But I'll be right back. Excuse me.

                    STEVE
All right.
                    (To HIMSELF.)
Law's about going into a house…. What the hell is wrong with this state?
                    (As STEVE waits for HER to come back out. HE
                    wipes the sweat from HIS forehead. HE looks
                    around as HE looks down HE notices a cigarette
                    lying on the ground. HE picks it up and lights it.)
Damn hot out… fucking town.
                    (HE walks over to the grave.)
No date, no name, no nothing…. only a cross, poor as dirt.
                    (HE put his ashes from the cigarette out on the
                    cross then pulls a flask out and takes a swig from it.
                    HE pulls HIS camera out from his bag and takes a
                    photo of the grave. VIVIAN comes out of the
                    house a little cleaner.)

                    VIVIAN
(Seeing STEVE taking photos of the grave
disturbs HER.
What are you doing?

                    SHE starts to walk over there in distress
                    from what HE is doing. STEVE realizing
                    this turns around facing VIVIAN to get a
                    quick reaction shot.)

                    STEVE
It's all about manipulation…. of the subject that is. I probably got better shots of you giving me so many different emotions than I ever got from anyone else.
                    (HE goes in and touches HER face with a kiss.)
You're like a muse.

                    VIVIAN
A muse?

STEVE

A Muse, is one of the goddesses who inspire the creation of literature and the arts. They were considered the source of the knowledge, related orally for centuries in the ancient culture that was contained in poetic lyrics and myths.
(HE starts to kiss HER neck.)
That's a compliment to a real woman who inspires creativity.

VIVIAN

We need to...

STEVE

Stop? Oh no. I never.

> HE continues to kiss HER neck. HE grabs HER leg and runs HIS hand up HER thigh.

VIVIAN

I need to... I need to...
(SHE falls into the seduction of HIM kissing HER. SHE leans into being held by HIM as HE continues to kiss. SHE pulls him close. Softly.)
Oh, Stop.
(SHE pulls away from HIM.)
I need to stop.

> HE steps back and holds HIS camera up. HE takes a shot.

STEVE

Damn! I'm out of film.

> HE walks off over to HIS bag and changes the film in HIS camera. SHE stands there trying to control HER urge.

VIVIAN

What the hell is happening to me?

STEVE
Pleasure. Do you ever masturbate?
(HE takes another photo.)

VIVIAN
What?

STEVE
What? Master… you know… pleasuring yourself?
(Takes another photo.)

VIVIAN
I really don't appreciate this.

STEVE
What, the question? Like that's worse than being asked to go sit in the back of the bus. It's healthy you know, sex… There is nothing wrong to discuss amongst adults.

VIVIAN
It's private.

STEVE
I won't alert the Associated Press.

VIVIAN
I have not had… not been with anyone
(SHE looks down.)
but my husband. I cannot…. it would be a sin.
(Another shot.)

STEVE
How about by yourself?

VIVIAN
No.

STEVE
Pent up, huh?
(Another shot.)

VIVIAN
'We' don't talk about that.

STEVE
It's funny how a lot of people refuse to talk about pleasure. You know you're a beautiful woman Vivian.

VIVIAN
I don't feel like that. I never have.

STEVE
Why?
(Another shot.)

VIVIAN
I guess I don't know how to feel beautiful.

STEVE
Why don't you sit down in that chair?

VIVIAN sits.

VIVIAN
Ok.

STEVE sits down across from HER in the other chair. HE kicks HIS shoe off and sticks HIS foot between HER legs. SHE tries to resist. VIVIAN is in a state of shock yet at the same time enjoys it. While this is going on STEVE takes few photos of HER. SHE moans. HE puts the camera down as this continues. HE pulls out HIS harmonica and starts to play. LIGHTS: Black out.

ACT ONE SCENE FOUR

AT RISE: VIVIAN is sleeping on a blanket on the ground outside. STEVE stands over HER with HIS back facing the audience. HE is holding the camera up taking a picture of HER sleeping.

STEVE

Shit!
>(HE turns around now facing the audience. HE shows that HE has shaving cream on one side of HIS face. HE looks up into the sky.)

I'm losing light. Damn.
>(HE steps over HER and goes back to the chair HE had been sitting in. In front of the chair is a bucket of water and a little mirror and a razor that HE had been using. HE starts to shave again. VIVIAN starts to wake up SHE opens HER eyes and looks around. Realizing where SHE is, SHE sits up real quick.)

Good evening, Vivian.

VIVIAN

Good evening.
>(SHE smiles.)

STEVE

Hello again.

VIVIAN

I slept. I can't believe it. I never sleep.

STEVE

The result of pure pleasure, perhaps?

VIVIAN

How long did I sleep?

STEVE
A while.
> (STEVE looks up into the sky.)

Three hours, maybe.

VIVIAN
And you just… What did you do?

STEVE
I…
> (HE smirks out of embarrassment.)

…laid next to you.
> (HE looks over at HER, SHE looks away.)

VIVIAN
What are you doing?

STEVE
Shaving.

VIVIAN
Oh, ok.

STEVE
You don't mind, do you?
> (HE finishes shaving and puts HIS hands in the bucket and splashes water on HIS face.)

VIVIAN
Of course not.
> (HE walks over to HER and sits down on the blanket.)

Oh, hi.
> (SHE kisses HIM.)

STEVE
Hi again. How are you? Are you okay?

VIVIAN
I um… yes I don't know.
(SHE laughs)

STEVE
Laughing is good.

VIVIAN
Yes…. When do you leave?

STEVE
Why, are you trying to get rid of me?

VIVIAN
No. No. Just…

STEVE
It's okay.

VIVIAN
When do you go back to New York?

STEVE
Ah my city, you should go someday.

VIVIAN
I don't know what I would do there.

STEVE
Let me ask you something? Do you like it here?

VIVIAN
What's it like there?

STEVE
What's it like there? Hmmm God what's it like there?

VIVIAN
Do you mind not saying his name like that?

STEVE
What God?

VIVIAN
Yes.

STEVE
God? Are you serious?

VIVIAN
I already asked you please. Could you not take the name of our lord and savior in vain?

STEVE
Ok, sorry. You're a religious girl, huh?

VIVIAN
Is there any other way?

STEVE
(HE shrugs.)
I don't know. There's hookers... How... How do you feel about God taking your husband away?
(SHE puts HER head down.)

VIVIAN
There's a reason for that.

STEVE
What's that reason?

VIVIAN
It's getting late.
> (SHE goes to stand up. HE grabs HER by the arm and pulls her back down.)

You should best... um, probably be going.

STEVE
In my experience New York it's the 'only city'. It's the only city where you can be walking amongst hundreds of people and yet still be more alone, more distant, more private than anywhere else imaginable. In New York people mind their own business. Not like the people appear to be down here. No matter what your background, from culture to art to food you can be worldly without ever leaving the city. From film to music to architecture to booze...
> (STEVE pulls HIS flask out.)

...to the alleyway where the bums sleep New York has it all.
> (HE takes a swig out of HIS flask.)

VIVIAN
Do you think you drink a lot?

STEVE
Only when I'm thirsty. What was I talking about? To...

VIVIAN
It. Sounds...

STEVE
Sorry, I'm rambling. I try to come up with some kind of answer as oppose to just saying the city "it's great"! How about here?

VIVIAN
Here?

STEVE
Yeah, what do you do here?

                    VIVIAN
I… it's really great.

                    STEVE
It's great.

                    VIVIAN
Yes.

                    STEVE
Is that before or after the cross burning parties that happen around here.

                    VIVIAN
It's fine… It's horrible, it's horrible.

                    STEVE
Why don't you leave this place?

                    VIVIAN
To go where and do what?

                    STEVE
The city has everything and anything.

                    VIVIAN
Do you have family back in New York?

                    STEVE
Family ah... That's a story for another day.
          (HE reaches out and touches HER breast.)

                    VIVIAN
Stop.

STEVE

Why?
(STEVE takes HER hand and puts it on HIS face.
VIVIAN takes HIS hand and starts to suck on HIS
fingers.)
Can I have some more of you?
(VIVIAN goes to unbutton HER shirt but SHE
stops.)

VIVIAN
Do you think this is right?

STEVE
Yes.

VIVIAN
Do I dare say, "My righteousness is more than god's"? It's not. It can't be.

STEVE
You talk to god a lot, don't you?

VIVIAN
He's what I need to go about my day. You are only passing through. I still need to live with myself afterwards. I already have to live with what just happened.

STEVE
You didn't go all the way.

VIVIAN
Went close enough and far enough.

STEVE
You have a child, don't you?

VIVIAN
Yes. You know I do.

STEVE
Were you already married when you had the child?

VIVIAN
(SHE turns away.)
No. That's a story for another day…

STEVE
I'm sure that god didn't like that.

VIVIAN
That's not funny. I ask you please. It's what I have.

STEVE
So tell me…
    (Pointing at the grave stone.)
…what was his secret of getting you.

VIVIAN
I'm not feeling too good. You need to go. I need to go in.

STEVE
Have you ever gone out to dinner?

VIVIAN
No.

STEVE
Could I take you? Would you like to go? That's a normal okay thing to do… in the eyes of god?

VIVIAN
Yes but not in the eyes that live in this town.

STEVE
That's a clever one.

VIVIAN
I cannot be seen with you, this is bad enough.

STEVE
So I guess a movie is out of the question. No Sammy Davis Jr.?

VIVIAN
I must be crazy. This has already gone out of control.

STEVE
Or maybe you're one brave girl. I like… I want… no… I 'need' to see you again.

VIVIAN
Tell me, why am I not saying no when I know should?

STEVE
So then, just say "No" so you did say no. I'll show up again anyway.

VIVIAN
Yes.

STEVE
I'll bring lunch, is there anything you're allergic to?

VIVIAN
Yes, you. What am I saying?

STEVE
I'm contagious… You're not dumb, Vivian.

VIVIAN
I am. I know I am.

STEVE
No, just stuck.

VIVIAN
Are we saying goodbye?

STEVE
How?

VIVIAN
I don't know how.

STEVE
I'll keep things tame for you and god, the rest of the night.
(HE blows HER a kiss, SHE smiles.)

VIVIAN
Have a good night.

STEVE
Yes, you too.
(STEVE turns around and rolls HIS eyes.)

ACT ONE SCENE FIVE

AT RISE: Inside VIVIAN'S house.

VIVIAN
Yes. Yes! What am I saying… why can't I control myself? Lord, are you testing me? If so, I failed again. You're behind me.

SON
Yeah, ma'am.

VIVIAN
It's yes.
    (SHE turns around.)
Have you been fighting again?

SON
No, ma'am.

VIVIAN
So if I turn around, you won't be bloody again?

SON
No ma'am.

VIVIAN
Did you not go to school again?

SON
No, sorry.

VIVIAN
You need to go to school. You need to get an education. Please …You cannot be like…
    (Pause.)
…your father.

SON
The schools don't want us educated.

VIVIAN
God helps those that help themselves. We get what we can from what is offered.

SON
That's why you never read to me when I was a child.

VIVIAN
Are you hungry?

SON
Yes. Is that what you are offering?

VIVIAN
I'll make you something.

STEVE enters.

STEVE
Can you make me something too?

VIVIAN
What are you doing here?

The SON looks at HER startled.

STEVE
I left my cigarettes outside.

VIVIAN
That's outside, not in here.

STEVE
Wow! You get tough in public. Is she always like this kid?

VIVIAN
Don't talk to him! You have no right to be here. You have no right to intrude on my life.

STEVE
So being that I'm not allowed to talk to your son, and being that the cigarettes are not outside where I left them, maybe you can ask him if he has them.

SON
Sorry sir. I did not know they was yours... I'm a really sorry, Sir.

STEVE
It's alright kid.
    (To VIVIAN.)
Are you still angry?

VIVIAN
Angry. Yes I'm angry! I am angry that this son I had, wants to do everything that I ask him not to. He's turning into his father.
    (Turning to HER son.)
...into your father. You want to smoke and not go to school. You want to chase all them girls around, don't you? You're turning into one of them.

STEVE
Jesus Christ!

VIVIAN
What did I ask you not to say?

SON
She hates that, mister.

VIVIAN
Don't talk to him. Go outside!

STEVE
I just thought it was God, now it's Jesus Christ also. Anybody else I can't say? How about Fidel Castro? Is his name off limits too?

VIVIAN
(To the SON.)
Go outside! And cigarettes now!
(The SON hands HER the cigarettes and exits.)
And you…

STEVE
May I enter?

VIVIAN
Might as well, you're already half in as it is.

STEVE
I'm looking to go all the way.

VIVIAN
Pardon? What's next? Is that baby boy going to come home drunk? I don't know.

STEVE
Take it easy, alright?
(HE touches HER face.)

VIVIAN
I can't do this with you anymore. I can't see…
(Pauses.)

STEVE
You know, I think I'm going outside and have a talk with your son.

VIVIAN
I'd rather you not.

                    STEVE
I'm going to anyway. Cigs?

                    VIVIAN
Huh?

                    STEVE
Cigarettes baby. No kiss?
          (SHE hands HIM the cigarettes.)
It's a free country, and all.
          (STEVE exits.)

                    VIVIAN
What a rumor that is.

                    The SON is sitting on the porch uneasy
                    when STEVE approaches HIM. HE sits next
                    to HIM.

                    STEVE
How you doing, kid?

                    SON
Um...
          (Nervous.)
Fine.

                    STEVE
Do you smoke?
          (HE looks up at STEVE who puts one in HIS own
          mouth.)
Go ahead… take one I won't tell if you don't.
          (The SON takes a cigarette.)
You still have my lighter?

SON

Sorry mister, I's didn't know they was yours.
>(HE hands STEVE the lighter. STEVE stops HIM and the SON lights the cigarette for HIM and then HIS own.)

STEVE

Keep it. I have another one back at that motel in town.

SON

Really? I can keep it?

STEVE
>(HE takes out HIS flask and takes a shot.)

Quit the act, kid. Seriously. How old are you?

SON

Twelve.

STEVE

That's good enough in my book... You want a shot?
>(The SON looks at him.)

I won't tell if you don't.
>(The SON takes the flask and downs it.)

Whoa! Hey now....
>(STEVE takes it from HIM.)

Not too much now. You don't want her to smell it on your breath.

SON

She's looking out at us, right now.
>(STEVE looks in HER direction.)

STEVE

Perhaps a wave...
>(HE waves.)

and just smile... there she goes.

SON
That worked!

STEVE
Yeah.
(HE smiles.)
...You like it around here?

SON
It's not anything.

STEVE
It's too hot around here

SON
It's not anything.

STEVE
It's too segregated around here for me.
(HE laughs.)
That's a word I never thought I use in a sentence "It's too segregated here for me".
(Laughs)
Oh God! Take another shot kid.
(STEVE takes a shot then passes it to the SON.)

SON
Thanks, mister.

STEVE
Mister... Whoa ... my name is Steve. Put it their kid... It sure is peaceful around here, though.

SON
Yeah, I guess it is when the whites are not stirring up trouble.
(Realizing whom HE is talking to.)
Oh, sorry, I did not mean that.

STEVE
The whites around here cause a lot of trouble, huh?
>(The SON stares at HIM. HE hands HIM the flask again.)

SON
Where are you from, Steve?

STEVE
First, let me get another shot of that.
>(HE takes the flask.)
New York, kid.

SON
New York? Wow! What are you doing all away out here?

STEVE
Working.

SON
Working? What are you…

STEVE
>(Interrupts.)
I'm a photographer. I take pictures.

SON
Oh. Is that what you're doing here tonight?

STEVE
Yeah. I was taking some photographs of your
>(Pause.)
mother.

SON
Makes sense, why else would you be talking to her.

STEVE
Do you like girls, kid?

SON
Yeah.
(Takes a shot from the flask.)

STEVE
You make love to one of them yet?

SON
What no! I can't.

> STEVE takes the flask again and takes a shot.

STEVE
You can't...
(STEVE laughs.)
Why?

SON
Mom says it's a sin before marriage.

STEVE
A sin, meaning you would go to hell instead of heaven?

SON
Yes, sir.

STEVE
Well kid...
(HE hands HIM the flask.)
...you can finish it. Well kid, if you wait until you're married then die and go to heaven, you may be very lonely up there as everyone else will be down in hell.

                    SON
Steve, you make love to any of them yet?

                    STEVE
Yeah man! My first one was a prostitute.

                    SON
A prostitute? You paid for it. Oh my god!

                    STEVE
Yeah, only way to do it the first time, go for a pro, less awkward.

                    SON
People would look down at me for that in this town... They already do anyway.

                    STEVE
Hell with those people.

                    SON
Yeah. How do you get the girls?

                    STEVE
My profession helps.

                    SON
How's that?

                    STEVE
Any girl... any woman would love to think that they have some kind of beauty that you would love to take the time to capture with this...

>   STEVE pulls HIS camera out and hands it to the SON.

SON
That's nice.

STEVE
Yep. This is the Kodak Color Snap 35. It came out last year.

SON
Can I take a picture?

STEVE
It's too dark, you wouldn't see anything.

SON
Oh, okay.

STEVE
Ah hell! Take a photo anyway. Press that button on the top.

SON
That one?

STEVE
Yeah, that one.

SON
Smile.
    (HE takes a photo of STEVE who does not smile.)
This helps to get girls?

STEVE
Yeah, just let me have that back now.
    (The SON hands it back to HIM)
Just say to a girl you like, "Wow there is something about you… Wow! What is it? I would love to photograph you". It's easy… charm her… Anything left in that flask?

SON
Sorry, you said I could finish what was left.

STEVE
No… you're right. I did say that. So as you're photographing her, romanticize it. Be like nothing else is important but her. …It's about that beauty of theirs that you must capture… Anything else is not of importance. Only her… That rare beauty she has that you never, ever witness before and probably will never, not ever see again… Ha! I need a beer!
(STEVE pulls a beer out of HIS bag.)
Its' a come on… You know just romance them kid. Make yourself believe it, within your own mind, without overdoing it. But… ah! Every once in a while…. no not every once in a while but one time in your life it could become real, you may not know it at first. Real emotions. To the small surprises you didn't know you had in you.

> STEVE takes a drink of HIS beer, drops the can as LIGHTS: Go down.

ACT ONE SCENE SIX

AT RISE: LIGHTS: Quickly come back up. The SON is
gone and VIVIAN is standing there.

VIVIAN
You need to leave. I'm sorry but I just don't know what "this" is.

STEVE
It's a pursuit that keeps stopping and backing up.

VIVIAN
You're drunk!

STEVE
Only buzzed.

VIVIAN
Why are you after me?

STEVE
You make it seem like it's a bad thing.

VIVIAN
I'm not anything special.

STEVE
Neither am I. But I know what that feeling is kicking around in my chest that feeling of nervous excitement driving back up here just to see you again this morning.

> STEVE puts HIS arms around HER from behind. HE holds HER and SHE sinks back into HIS chest.

VIVIAN
My son is inside.

STEVE
He won't come out here.

VIVIAN
How do you know that?

STEVE
It's a guy thing. You smell good again... still.

VIVIAN
No, I don't... Do I?

STEVE
How could you not?
>(SHE smiles. HE takes a sip out of HIS beer. SHE takes the can from HIM and takes a sip.)

Nice sky out here tonight.

VIVIAN
Yes, it is. I tell you no matter how I feel about my life. I can still look up and for that moment I feel at peace and wonder, a wonder that maybe my life can be more.

STEVE
You should see this sky from Central Park. That's in New York. It's amazing.

VIVIAN
How come I keep saying 'no more' and then I'm back in your arms?

STEVE
That's because the heart is stronger.
>(HE starts to put HIS arms all over HER and kisses HER.

VIVIAN
Stop it! Stop it! Stop!

STEVE
Stop?

VIVIAN
Stop …when you're done.
> (THEY lower THEMSELVES to the dirt, with HIM straddling atop HER.)

Wait…. my son.

STEVE
He won't come out.

VIVIAN
How can you be so sure?

STEVE
A man just… knows.

VIVIAN
Can you do that thing that you did before?
> (SHE moans.)

STEVE
Look at that sky.

> LIGHTS: Go out on them.

ACT TWO SCENE ONE

AT RISE: LIGHTS: Come up on the house. The SON stands
looking out on THEM. HE puts HIS head down
and walks back inside. LIGHTS: Black out during
which the voice of another woman is heard.

WOMAN
Steve! Where is Steve? I know he's been here.

> A sound is heard of someone hitting the
> floor. LIGHTS: Come up. VIVIAN and
> HER SON are on the porch standing over a
> young white WOMAN who appears to be
> passed out. The SON is poking HER with a
> stick.

VIVIAN
She breathing?

SON
She's breathing.

VIVIAN
Stop poking at her, boy. Go get Mr. Chaney.

SON
It's not doing anything bad to her.

VIVIAN
Because I told you to!

SON
That doesn't mean I'm going to stop. Mom what's
that…She's got cuts all over her arms.

VIVIAN
Will you stop poking her with that stick...
>   (Rips the stick out of HIS hand.)
...and go get Mr. Chaney, boy!

> HE raises HIS hand up as if HE is going to hit HER and VIVIAN jumps back in fear. HE puts HIS hand down and laughs. HE picks up the stick.

SON
I don't have to take this.

> HE walks off stage. VIVIAN stands there staring at HIM as HE goes.

VIVIAN
You are your father's son.
>   (To HERSELF)
Stop it.
>   (The WOMAN makes a noise.)
Ma'am, you ok?
>   (SHE doesn't know if SHE should touch HER.)
Ma'am?

WOMAN
>   (Out of it)
Where is.....

VIVIAN
Ma'am, can I get you a doctor or something?

WOMAN
He left me to rot.... Oh.... my eyes are on fire.

VIVIAN
Ma'am can I get you a doctor?

>   VIVIAN reaches down to help the
>   WOMAN, the WOMAN jumps up.

>   WOMAN

Don't touch me!

>   VIVIAN

I'm sorry... so sorry.

>   WOMAN

I...
>   (The WOMAN starts to dry heave)
It's bright... the light...

>   VIVIAN

It's morning ma'am.

>   WOMAN

Where have I been? It's morning.... it's this place... here! You're colored.
>   (SHE sniffs HER shirt that SHE has on.)
I have to....
>   (SHE pulls HER underwear off, sits back on the
>   floor.)
These are not mine.

>   VIVIAN
>   (VIVIAN not knowing how to handle this.)
Are you sick? Can I get you a doctor?

>   WOMAN

No, I am just going to the bathroom.
>   (SHE starts looking around at HER surroundings
>   and HER face shows that SHE recognizes things.)
It's this place. He's been here.
>   (SHE starts to crawl on HER hands to the steps of
>   the porch HER panties still wrapped in HER
>   hand.)

VIVIAN
Can I help you?

WOMEN
(SHE manages to get up on the steps and sits.)
The man whose foot was between your legs!
(SHE starts to dry heave again.)

VIVIAN
Oh no, he's married.... Oh, I am.... I did not know! Please can I help you? How do you know?
(VIVIAN goes to help the WOMAN. The
WOMAN collapses in HER arms.)
What is it that happened to you?

WOMAN
Love. I need some please! My skin is... it's like spiders crawling....

VIVIAN
Love?

WOMAN
Junk!

VIVIAN
Excuse me?

WOMAN
Junk!

VIVIAN
I do not know what that is?

WOMAN
Steve! Where is Steve? I saw the photos of you in his motel room. He wasn't there but you were all over his walls.

VIVIAN

I don't know what to say... Please, this was not my doing.

WOMAN

Why did he turn me into this but not you? Oh! My arms are itching.

VIVIAN

You have cuts all over your arms... best not scratch it. Let me get you to the table. Please stop scratching. Okay, I'm going to help you.
>(The WOMAN starts to dry heave, VIVIAN gets HER to the table.)

Please have some of this.
>(SHE picks up a cup)

Its water in here.... Drink some...
>(The WOMAN knocks the cup out of VIVIAN'S hand.)

WOMAN

What are you?

VIVIAN

Pardon, what am I?

WOMAN

I know this... I know this how... You must feel you're better than me. Getting him! He destroyed me you know. I was pretty... so pretty. Good lord my skin is burning up again. This man having a beer one night.... At, what was the name of the bar?... He says he's from New York; he's a photographer. I'm so pretty he said. I knew that, I said. He said, I'm more than just pretty. He needs to 'capture me'. I smiled.
>(SHE starts to dry heave again and grabbing at her clothes.)

Fuck, it's hot! We made love, not sex; love.

WOMAN (Cont'd)
He told me to come back to New York with him, I'm his muse. I wanted out of this going nowhere town. I'm better than the rest of you all! I told them all I'd be leaving one day. When was that day going to happen? Then he was here to make that day come to be. And then he said, 'I don't know if you should come back!' What can I do to go? "Take this" he says it's called 'smack'. "Let me photograph while you're taking it. You would be number one in my book for life if you would". Smack! So, who are you? Wait, I've seen you 'round. Your husband's dead right? He worked at the gas station in town?

VIVIAN
Yes, ma'am.

WOMAN
Hmmm! You always walk with your head down.
(VIVIAN looks up at HER.)
He photographed me shooting up all the time. He would say, "That's my number one girl. Tomorrow we leave for New York. But for now stick this needle in your arm baby. Create art for me by putting this needle in your arm for me".

VIVIAN
Did he do that to himself to?

WOMAN
No! Only to me! And then he left me one day.
(Looking at HER arms.)
I need to cover these up. He drove me to another state saying, "Tomorrow we'll be in New York" and he left me. He turned me into this!
(The WOMAN slams HER head on the table violently a number of times.)

                    WOMAN (Cont'd)
I went from playing bridge with the girls and going out to
dinner with good-looking boys who couldn't have me but
whose money I could have them spend on me, to screwing
men just to get back here. Back to this 'God awful' town!
Now... now I'm like you. I should just be of your color.

                    VIVIAN
              (SHE looks up.)
Excuse me how are you like me?

                    WOMAN
What?

                    VIVIAN
How are we alike?

                    WOMAN
We're on the same level now.
              (SHE stands up.)
When will Steve be here? I still... I'm sure he will still take
me back with him.

                    VIVIAN
Oh Lord please gives me my strength, because I just ran out
of hope for this place. You compare your actions to my skin
color. I go to church! I provide for my child alone! And you
ran off with the devil himself. We are not the same. You
were thrown away like a DOG.

                    WOMAN
I am not a dog!
              (SHE puts HER arms around VIVIAN'S throat.
              VIVIAN tries to fight back but can't get HER off
              HER back. SHE panics.)
You whore, you stole him from me! You god dam whore.

                    VIVIAN
Please, stop it!
          (VIVIAN falls to the ground the WOMAN still on
          top of HER. VIVIAN now starts to have a
          flashback.)
Please? I'm sorry. I'm sorry don't …
          (The WOMAN starts to get on top of HER and
          chokes HER.)
I can't do this.

                    WOMAN
I don't care.

          VIVIAN tries to reach for a rock.

                    VIVIAN
I'm a virgin! I'm a virgin! I'm a good girl.
          (SHE gets the rock and hits the WOMAN on the
          head with it. The WOMAN falls off of HER. SHE
          sits up.)
I'm a virgin I don't care that you're my husband!

                    SHE sits there in shock for a moment in
                    deep thought. She stares at the rock.
                    LIGHTS: Black out.

ACT TWO SCENE TWO

AT RISE: LIGHTS: Come up. VIVIAN is still sitting there
with that shocked look on HER face. The
WOMAN is in the house. SOUND: birds chirping.
SHE looks up into the sky closing HER eyes.
VIVIAN'S face begins to smile. JAMES enters.

JAMES
Miss Vivian. Miss Vivian? Vivian.
      (HE touches HER.)

VIVIAN
I'm sorry. Huh? Oh Mr. Chaney, where is she? Is she ok?

JAMES
She's fine… just a bump on her head. She's in the house. I
did not know what else to do with her. This is not good.

VIVIAN
I can't believe what I did.

JAMES
Here, have some coffee.
      (HE hands HER a cup.)

VIVIAN
Thank you. Thank you for your help Mr. Chaney. You've
been very good to us.

JAMES
How could I not be good to you, Miss Vivian?

VIVIAN
I cannot believe how I acted. That tortured woman showed
up looking for some man and I am so, so stupid I…

JAMES
No, you're not stupid.

VIVIAN
I acted so... what's the word? I was not 'me' today. This... I don't know who I am anymore... maybe I'm growing? I don't want to be that person I was today. I lost it... if only for a second.

JAMES
Listen Miss Vivian. Vivian?
> (HE touches HER shoulder. SHE looks up.)

I know you for many years. I was a good friend of your husband.

VIVIAN
Yes I know.

JAMES
I know how he got you young, it wasn't right. He wasn't always right. I wish I could have done something about it at the time. I should have. I'm sorry. I want you to know that no matter what happens to you and what you're going through at the moment, I'll always be here for you. I'll always be good and kind to you. I'm just... I don't know how to... I just want to take you out sometime soon, on a date, sometime soon. Tomorrow would be good for me. I don't have anything to do tomorrow except work... and I am off the following day after work.

VIVIAN
I would like that.

JAMES
Really?

VIVIAN
Yes.

JAMES
I had wanted to ask you that for the longest time.

VIVIAN
Here he comes.

JAMES
Huh?

VIVIAN
That man.

JAMES
I'll deal with this.

VIVIAN
No, please!
(Calms down.)
It's okay. I can take care of this. Why don't you go home for now, I'll see you tomorrow.

JAMES
I'd rather stay.

VIVIAN
James please, I don't want you thinking any different of me. Please come back though. I would like it if you could come by later.

JAMES
I hope you know what you're doing Miss Vivian... Vivian? I hope you know what to do.

JAMES walks off.

VIVIAN
Knowing what to do and what you're doing have always collided with me.

STEVE enters.

STEVE

Hi.

VIVIAN
I don't know what to think of you.

STEVE

Where is she?

VIVIAN
In the house. I hit her with a rock.

STEVE
She… Um yeah, I'll go in, is that ok?

> VIVIAN walks over to the tombstone.

VIVIAN

You broke that girl.

> STEVE walks over to HER and picks HER up. VIVIAN is stunned by this. STEVE walks HER over to the chair and places HER in it. HE then touches HER face.

STEVE
She was on the verge of breaking; I just tipped her over.

> STEVE walks up the steps into the house.

VIVIAN
I may have been seduced by the devil himself.

> VIVIAN gets out of the chair. HER body moves in pain towards the tombstone.

VIVIAN (Cont'd)

I don't know what to do anymore. I always felt I needed to escape from you. Now I feel I need to escape from this world. You raped me. You did! I said no, I am sure, to you. I said no. I did! All that's needed to say, I did. You raped me and left me with a child, whom I'm afraid is turning into you. Another degenerate....

> While this is going on, STEVE has already exited the house and walked towards HER. SHE realizes HE is behind HER and turns around.

STEVE

You might as well keep going. You've already said it.

VIVIAN

Why do I say degenerate? A mother should not think that of her own flesh? Maybe it's the misery I went through every day of my life from that night on. That boy is what I have to show from it. Maybe he looks like you. Maybe he's starting to act like you. Maybe this it's a dream and I'll wake up in my mother's arms and be the age of fourteen again. (Steve holds her hand) I... I am exhausted. I am holding a hand and I don't even know you and I've done...

STEVE

Who 'really knows' anybody?

VIVIAN

And that...girl?

STEVE

It's fine. I'll get her out of here. She's just an addict.

VIVIAN

You seduced her?

STEVE

You know sex can be a fun pleasure too, Vivian. It's not always the way you're thinking about it. You are allowed to say 'yes' sometimes. It's allowed in the world.

VIVIAN

Not in "this world" here with you.
(SHE lets go of HIS hand.)
These emotions are too much to handle right now.

STEVE

Say you'll come to New York with me.

VIVIAN

New York? I have a son to… you know a son.

STEVE

You hate him.

VIVIAN

I have a son.

STEVE

Do you want to stay here and suffer in your bad memories?

VIVIAN

Like you know anything about it?

STEVE

Hell everyone has suffered. I wish that you would have met my mother, she was a piece of work. You have never met a more self-absorbed women in my life. I remember a time I was sick, she made me lay on the floor that whole day because she did not want my germs on the furniture. But her dirty dogs were good enough for furniture. Another time I became sick at a family Christmas party, she made me go sleep in the car in the dead of winter.

STEVE (Cont'd)
I threw up in the driveway and in my sick state she thought it would be more important for me clean the driveway instead of going to bed. You see her mindset developing over the years from laying on the floor to going into the car. I had strep throat she had me walk to the hospital. The best was when she walked in on me masturbating and decided to bring it up at dinner in front of her friends. When I was a kid, I asked her if I was good-looking and she just laughed. Now, I never was raped and I never suffered from being criticized about the color of my skin but… but we all had suffering in our lives. One-way or another we have. Damn it… Wow! I need a drink.

VIVIAN
I am going for a walk. Please, be gone.

STEVE
That's it?

VIVIAN
This is. I am sorry for your own problems.

VIVIAN exits.

STEVE
I poured out my soul. What the hell?
(STEVE looks up into the sky. HE puts a cigarette in HIS mouth.)
Yeah!

LIGHTS: Black out.

ACT TWO SCENE THREE

AT RISE: LIGHTS: Come up. STEVE walks over to HIS bag and pulls out a little case which contains a syringe. HE then puts the syringe back in the case and walks into the house. A few seconds later the WOMAN is tossed out of the house onto the ground.

WOMAN

Awwwwww!

> The WOMAN starts to cry. STEVE walks out of the house.

STEVE

You cause enough trouble you fucking junkie.

> HE kicks HER in the stomach.

WOMAN

There is nothing more you can do to me, Steve!

STEVE

There's always more.
(HE stands HER up.)
It's ok. It's ok.
(HE punches HER in the face.)
And now for pleasure.
(HE takes HER arm.)
Pulse. There it is.
(HE injects the syringe into HER arm. HE lets HER go. SHE falls onto the ground. HE kicks HER one more time.)

WOMAN

Please. Oh. Yes.

STEVE now carries HER into the house and places HER on the rug and comes walking back out. STEVE then goes to the bag and pulls out HIS camera.

STEVE
Oh, hey there you are. Come over here.

The SON comes on stage.

SON
Everything all right with that white girl, Steve?

STEVE
Yea man just a bit too much to drink. Thanks for coming into town to get me that was damn right decent of you.
(HE pulls out the flask.)
Here man, have a shot.

SON
Where is…

STEVE
Your mother's not here.
(Hands the flask to HIM.)
She won't be back for a while.
(The SON takes a shot and goes to hand it back to HIM.)
No take another shot.

SON
Alright.
(Takes another shot.)
Thanks, Steve.

                    STEVE
Not a problem buddy… Now it's time for the boy to become
a man. Why don't you go have sex with that girl inside?
          (The SON stands there stunned as STEVE takes a
          photo.)
Take another shot from the flask.

                    SON
The white girl?

          STEVE continues to photograph.

                    STEVE
Yeah, she's in there waiting for you.

                    SON
That's um… She's a white girl that just doesn't happen
around here.

                    STEVE
But it should. You can be the first. What better way to have
your first time but by doing it to someone who thinks they're
better then you. By taking that away from them in the most
emotional way. You do like girl's right?

                    SON
Yeah! I do.

                    STEVE
Then go. I'll be lookout for you. You are about to be a man.
Take the flask in with you. You can have the rest.

          HE continues to photograph the SON as HE
          walks into the house.

                    SON
You're a good friend.

STEVE
You're a good kid. Excuse me. You're a good man. And remember this is between us. Now go in and enter her.

> The SON enters the house. LIGHTS: Come up in the house to see the WOMAN lying there. The SON awkwardly pulls HIS pants down and gets on top of HER. LIGHTS: Black out on the house.

STEVE
Oh yeah, what a world we live in! What a world!

> LIGHTS: Black out.

ACT TWO SCENE FOUR

AT RISE: LIGHTS: Come up. VIVIAN enters with a bag of
groceries. SHE walks up the steps onto the porch.
As SHE walks into the house SHE sees HER SON
lying on top of the white WOMAN and stops
dropping the groceries on the ground.

VIVIAN
What are you doing?

> SHE quickly walks down the steps of the
> house. The SON runs out after HER pulling
> HIS pants up.

SON
Mom wait.

VIVIAN
No. I don't want to hear it.

SON
No, you'll wait!

> HE grabs HER and turns HER around. SHE
> slaps HIM as SHE turns.

VIVIAN
What kind of boy are you!

SON
I am not no boy anymore. I do what I want.

VIVIAN
That white woman was bleeding.
> (SHE slaps HIM again.)

You are your father.

                        SON
You're nothing of a mother. Now don't talk to me like that.
Woman, go inside and make me dinner.

                        VIVIAN
Don't talk to me like that. You are twelve years old. You are
not a man, you are a child. Now you listen to me....
            (HE punches HER in the face. SHE stands there
            and takes it in stunned surprise. To HERSELF.)
Oh! Don't fall
            (SHE almost collapses but manages to stay up.)
There is nothing you can do to me that has not already been
done by what you came from.

                        SON
Shut up!
            (HE punches HER again. This time VIVIAN falls
            to the ground.)
I am not a what! I am not a what!
            (As this is going on STEVE watches from the
            corner smoking a cigarette as the SON kicks
            VIVIAN.)
I am your son! I'm your son. I'm...
            (HE starts to cry.)
I don't need you.

                    The SON runs off, as VIVIAN lies there
                    staring up.

                        VIVIAN
Rid me of this life please. Oh, oh...

                    STEVE walks over staring at HER.

                        STEVE
Oh, god.

VIVIAN
Oh, god. Rid me of this life, please.

STEVE
You got it. Lets clean you up
>(HE reaches HIS hand out, SHE does not take it.)

Ok.
>(HE picks HER up and sits HER down on a chair.)

I came back to get the girl. You're nose... here.
>(HE hands HER HIS handkerchief. SHE stares at HIM.)

What?

VIVIAN
You know you're not right in the head.

STEVE
Oh it's not the head I have the problems with it's the heart that I wish I could be rid of.

>SHE smacks HIM.

VIVIAN
Do you really want me?

STEVE
What?

VIVIAN
Do you really want me?

STEVE
Yes.

>VIVIAN sticks HER finger in HIS mouth.

VIVIAN
I hate you!

>   SHE pulls HIM closer to HIM and kisses
>   HIM.

STEVE

Hate and love go hand and hand…

>   HE pulls HER body onto HIS lap. As THEY
>   continue to kiss, SHE digs HER knee into
>   HIS and get up. SHE takes a couple steps
>   back still staring at HIM.

VIVIAN

Have me then.

>   STEVE walks over and touches HER face.
>   HE goes into kiss HER. SHE bites HIS lip
>   and pulls HIS hair.

VIVIAN

I want to forget about this place!

STEVE

No problem.

VIVIAN

I want to leave now!

STEVE

Anything.

VIVIAN

Put me over his grave.

STEVE

What?

VIVIAN

Do me over his tombstone!

> HE lifts HER up and carries HER to the tombstone. SHE continues to kiss him roughly. HE lets go of HER, HER legs land on the ground sitting on the tombstone. HE starts to unbutton HIS shirt. SHE slaps HIM again. HE glares at HER. SHE goes to slap HIM again, HE catches HER hand and with HIS other hand grabs HER by the neck. As HE lets go of HER hand, SHE unbuttons HIS pants and wraps HER legs around HIM.

VIVIAN
Why did this happen to me? I hate men! I hate them!

STEVE
Dig your nails into my back.

VIVIAN
What?

STEVE
I said, dig your nails into my fuckin' back.

> SHE does. THEY start to moan as THEY proceed.

VIVIAN
I...why did you do this to me! I can't take it. I... I love and hate you.

> SHE screams in pleasure, THEY kiss.
> LIGHTS: Black out.

ACT TWO SCENE FIVE

AT RISE: LIGHTS: Come back up. It's only a few minutes later. STEVE is pacing and smoking a cigarette. VIVIAN is leaning up on the tombstone.

STEVE
I have some of your blood on my shirt.

VIVIAN
What are we going to do about the white woman in my house?

STEVE
Let life deal with her. That's not our problem.

VIVIAN
What's going to happen?

STEVE
To her? Probably death.

VIVIAN
I mean us?

STEVE
Life and then death.

VIVIAN
Are we going to be happy?

STEVE
Are you going to be happy?

VIVIAN
Maybe, I hope. What is going to become of that boy I had?

STEVE
Not your problem.

VIVIAN
Isn't it?

STEVE
Husband rapes you, nine months later you have a son, that's insane. How are you supposed to be happy here? How am I supposed to be happy without you?

VIVIAN
I never been in anything like this before. I don't know if I know how be.

STEVE
Who knows anything?

VIVIAN
I need to pack.

STEVE
No, you don't. We'll get what we need on the way.

VIVIAN
I need to take a few things.

STEVE
Nothing you're going to need for a fresh start. I am going to start the car. Hurry up. We do need to rush out of here before that junkie wakes up.

VIVIAN
Hey.

STEVE
What?

VIVIAN
Kiss me? Just a kiss without anything else?

STEVE
Of course.
> (HE goes to kiss HER. As THEY politely kiss, HE starts to grab HER. SHE pushes HIM away.)

I always like a little bit more.
> (SHE puts HER head down.)

You are coming right?

VIVIAN
Yes.

STEVE
I'm going to start the car. You okay?

VIVIAN
I'm fine.

STEVE
If not for me, just remember a new life. Got that? Keep saying it a new life in New York, a new experience, a new journey, a new life.

VIVIAN
A new life... Yeah, I mean yes.

STEVE
See you in a minute.
> (As HE leaves, HE says to HIMSELF.)

I've won.

VIVIAN
In a minute.

> SHE puts HER head down again. For a second, SHE closes HER eyes and looks up

into the sky. SHE smiles again. SOUND: Birds chirping. SHE opens HER eyes and smile turns to misery again.

VIVIAN
Will I ever be able to find me? I can change him.
>(SHE walks inside the house and grabs HER purse and discovers the flask that is lying next to the white WOMAN in the house. SHE walks back out of the house.)

I think I am going to be sick.

>JAMES enters carrying flowers.

JAMES
Hello Miss Vivian!

VIVIAN
Oh Mr. Chaney.

JAMES
James please, how did everything go last night with that woman?

VIVIAN
Oh it's fine. Everything taken care of.

JAMES
Glad to hear it. I was nervous about the situation.

VIVIAN
No need to be.

JAMES
These are for you.
>(HE hands HER the flowers.)

I always think a lovely woman deserves some flowers on a beautiful day before church.

VIVIAN
Today's Sunday, I forgot.

JAMES
Looks like you got hit Miss Vivian, look at your mouth.
> (HE takes a step toward HER and touches HER face.)

VIVIAN
Oh it's nothing. I fell.

JAMES
You got some scratches and scrapes.

VIVIAN
Life is but scratches and scrapes, Mr. Chaney.

JAMES
Can I please escort you to church Miss Vivian? Excuse me Mrs. Vivian.

VIVIAN
It's Miss today.

JAMES
Please don't say no. I hate going by myself. It would be nice to go with a lovely person on such a beautiful day. Please don't say no.

VIVIAN
> (SHE looks down at STEVE'S flask.)

Yes.

JAMES

Really?

VIVIAN
I would love to.

JAMES
Oh that is… would be, excuse me, very nice.

VIVIAN
Do me a favor could you just place these flowers around back. There is a vase to put them in and we can be off.

JAMES
Sure, Miss Vivian, sure.

VIVIAN
Thank you.

JAMES
You really are a wonderful person, Miss Vivian.
>   (HE walks around back.)

VIVIAN
I wish I could have been.
>   (SHE picks HER pocketbook and runs offstage.
>   JAMES comes back on.)

JAMES
Oh, Miss Vivian, where did you say the vase was?
>   (HE looks out the sound of car door closes and a
>   car is heard driving off. You can see in HIS face
>   the pain that just overtook HIS heart. HE walks
>   over to the tombstone and drops the flowers.)

I guess we are both alone now.

LIGHTS: Fade out.

The End

If you have enjoyed this play, please leave a review on

amazon

and

Like Us On facebook

BLACK BOX THEATRE PUBLISHING

NOW AVAILABLE!!!

Poop Happens!" in this send up of all things cowboy!

So, Who Was That Masked Guy Anyway? is the story of Ernie, the grandson of the original Masked Cowboy, a lawman who fought for truth, justice and the cowboy way in the old west. Now that Grandpa is getting on in years he's looking for someone to carry on for him. The only problem? Ernie doesn't know anything about being a cowboy. He's never seen a real cow, he's allergic to milk and to tell the truth he doesn't know one end of a horse from another! So it's off to cowboy school to learn the basics of cowboyology. He'll learn to rope and ride, chew and spit and to develop the perfect "Yee-Haw!". And it's a good thing, because a band of no good outlaws have captured the good people of Gabby Gulch and the President of the United States, Theodore Roosevelt! Now it's up to Ernie and his friends to save the day...but beware, before it's all over, the poop is sure to hit the fans!

NOW AVAILABLE!!!

WANTED: SANTA CLAUS is the story of what happens when a group of department store moguls led by the greedy B. G. Bucks decide to replace Santa Claus with the shiny new "KRINGLE 3000", codenamed...ROBO-SANTA! A new Father Christmas with a titanium alloy outer shell housing a nuclear powered drive train, not to mention a snow white beard and a jolly disposition! These greedy tycoons will stop at nothing to get rid of jolly old St. Nick. That includes framing him for such crimes as purse snatching, tire theft and...oh no...not.....puppy kicking??!! Say it isn't so Santa! Now it's up to Santa's elves to save the day! But Santa's in no shape to take on his stainless steel counterpart! He'll have to train for his big comeback. Enter Mickey, one of the toughest elves of all time! He'll get Santa ready for the big showdown! But it's going to mean reaching deep down inside to find "the eye of the reindeer"!

NOW AVAILABLE!!!

At the edge of the universe sits The Long John Cafe. A place where the average guy and the average "Super" guy can sit and have a cup of coffee and just be themselves...or, someone else if that's what they want. The cafe is populated by iconic figures of the 20th Century, including cowboys, hippies, super heroes and movie stars. They've come to celebrate the end of the old Century and the beginning of tomorrow! That is, if they make it through the night! It seems the evil Dr. McNastiman has other plans for our heroes. Like their total destruction!

NOW AVAILABLE!!!

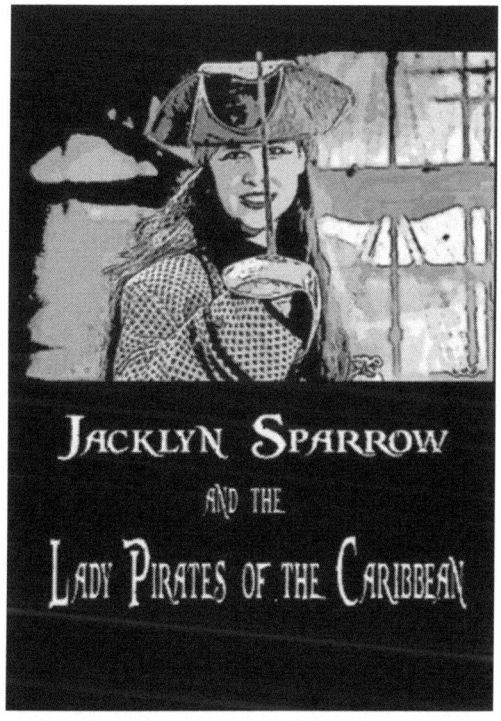

JACKLYN SPARROW AND THE LADY PIRATES OF THE CARIBBEAN

Why should the boys get to have all the fun?

Jacklyn Sparrow and the Lady Pirates of the Caribbean is our brand new swashbuckling pirate parody complete with bloodthirsty buccaneers in massive sword clanking battle scenes!! A giant wise cracking parrot named Polly!! Crazy obsessions with eye liner!! And just who is Robert, the Dreaded Phylum Porifera??

Of course the whole thing ends with a large celebration where everybody gets down with their bad selves!! It's fun for the whole family in this lampoon of everything you love about pirates!!!

NOW AVAILABLE!!!

"May the Dwarf be with you!"

A wacky take on the classic fairy tale which will have audiences rolling in the floor with laughter!

What happens when you mix an articulate mirror, a conceited queen, a prince dressed in purple, seven little people with personality issues, a basket of kumquats and a little Star Wars for good measure?

Snow White and the Seven Dwarves of the Old Republic!

NOW AVAILABLE!!!

Dear John
An ode to the potty.

"My dreams of thee flow softly.
They enter with tender rush.
The still soft sound which echoes,
When I lower the lid and flush."

They say that porcelain is the best antenna for creativity. At least that's what this cast of young people believe in Dear John: An ode to the potty! The action of this one act play takes place almost entirely behind the doors of five bathroom stalls. This short comedy is dedicated to all those term papers, funny pages and Charles Dickens' novels that have been read behind closed (stall) doors!

Bathroom humor at its finest!

NOW AVAILABLE!!!

**ELVIS MEETS NIXON
(OPERATION WIGGLE)**

Declassified after 40 years!

On December 21, 1970, an impromptu meeting took place between the King of Rock and Roll and the Leader of the Free World.

Elvis Meets Nixon (Operation Wiggle) is a short comedy which offers one possible (and ultimately ridiculous) explanation of what happened during that meeting.

NOW AVAILABLE!!!

Even Adam

In the beginning, there was a man.
Then there was a woman.
And then there was this piece of fruit...
...and that's when everything went horribly wrong!
Even Adam is a short comedy exploring the relationship
between men and women right from day one.

Why doesn't he ever bring her flowers like he used to?
Why doesn't she laugh at his jokes anymore?
And just who is that guy in the red suit?
And how did she convince him to eat that fruit, anyway?

NOW AVAILABLE!!!

THE DRACULA SPECTACULA

Count Dracula is bored. He's pretty much sucked Transylvania dry, and he's looking for a new challenge. So it's off to New York, New York! The Big Apple! The town that never sleeps...that'll pose a challenge for sure.
Dracula purchases The Carfax Theatre and decides to put on a big, flashy Broadway show...

THE DRACULA SPECTACULA!

Of course the Theatre just happens to be across the street from Dr. Seward's Mental Hospital where people have been mysteriously dying since The Count moved in.
Just a coincidence?
The play features a large cast of zany characters and is equal parts horror story and Broadway show spoof!

NOW AVAILABLE!!!

The FOUR PRESIDENTS

THE FOUR PRESIDENTS examines the lives and characters of four of the most colorful personalities to hold the office. Much of the dialogue comes from the Presidents' own words.

THE FARMER WHO WOULD BE KING presents George Washington through his own words, and the words of his biographer Mason Locke Weems. Was the father of our country a simple farmer who answered the call of his countrymen, or something more?

THE GREAT EMANCIPATOR is the story of a simple man. Born in the wilds of Kentucky and mostly self taught, Abraham Lincoln would someday be regarded as the greatest American who ever lived.

THE BULL MOOSE who occupied the White House 100 years ago was truly a man of action. Theodore Roosevelt was a father, author, rancher, sportsman, policeman, Rough Rider, cowboy, big game hunter, Governor of New York and eventually The President of the United States!

NIXON AND THE GHOSTS is a surreal drama with dialogue ripped straight from the headlines. On the night before his resignation, Nixon ponders his rise and fall, as the shadows themselves seem to come alive and he is confronted by the spirits of Presidents past!

NOW AVAILABLE!!!

The lights rise on a beautiful sunset.
A mermaid is silhouetted against an ocean backdrop.
Hauntingly familiar music fills the air.
Then...the Lawyer shows up.
And that's when the fun really begins!
The Little Mermaid (More or Less.) is the story of a Theatre company attempting to stage a children's version of the Hans Christian Anderson classic. The only problem? It looks and sounds an awful lot like a movie of the same name. That's when the Lawyer for a certain "mouse eared company" starts talking lawsuit for copyright infringement.
Lawsuit?
Copyright infringement?
Throw out the costumes!
What's that? There's a bunch of old clothes backstage from the 1970's? Well, don't just stand there! Go get them!
Ditch the music!
What? Somebody's mom has a greatest disco hits cd out in the car? That'll be perfect!
Change everyone's names!
Tartar Sauce! Little M.! The Crab Formerly Known as Sebastian!
Everybody ready? Ok...Action!!!

NOW AVAILABLE!!!

CINDERELLA
AND THE
QUEST FOR THE CRYSTAL PUMP

Adventure has a new name...

CINDERELLA!!!

Cinderella and the Quest for the Crystal Pump, is the story of a young girl seeking a life beyond the endless chores heaped upon her by her grouchy stepmother and two stepsisters.

Mow the grass! Beat the rugs! Churn the buttermilk!

Sometimes it's more than one girl can take!
More than anything, Cinderella wants to go to the prince's masquerade ball, but there's one problem...she has nothing to wear! Luckily, her Fairy Godperson has a few ideas.

Meanwhile, Prince Charles Edward Tiberius Charming III, or "Charlie" as he prefers to be called, has run away with his pals, Touchstone the Jester and the Magic Mirror, searching for a quiet place where he can just enjoy a good book!

Now this mismatched quartet find themselves on a quest to find the greatest treasure of all...the perfect pair of Crystal Pumps!

NOW AVAILABLE!!!

SHORESPEARE

Shorespeare is loosely based on a Midsummer Night's Dream. Shakespeare, with the help of Cupid, has landed at the Jersey Shore. Cupid inspires him to write a play about two New Jersey sweethearts, Cleo and Toni. Shakespeare is put off by their accent and way of talking, but decides to send the two teenagers on a course of true love. Toni and Cleo are determined to get married right after they graduate from high school, but in order to do so they must pass this course of true love that Cupid's pixies create and manipulate. As they travel along the boardwalk at the Jersey Shore, Cleo and Toni, meet a handful of historical figures disguised as the carnies. Confucius teaches Cleo the "Zen of Snoring", Charles Ponzi teaches them the importance of "White Lies", Leonardo Da Vinci shows them the "Art of Multitasking", and finally they meet Napolean who tries to help them to "Accept Shortcomings" of each other. After going through all these lessons, the sweethearts decide that marriage should wait, and Cupid is proud of Shakespeare who has finally reached out to the modern youth.

NOW AVAILABLE!!!

Everyone has heard the phrase, "it's the squeaky wheel that gets the oil," but how many people know the Back-story? The story begins in a kingdom far, far away over the rainbow – a kingdom called Spokend. This kingdom of wheels is a happy one for the gods have blessed the tiny hamlet with plentiful sunshine, water and most important –oil. Until a terrible drought starts to dry up all the oil supplies. What is to be done?

The powerful barons of industry and politicians decide to hold a meeting to decide how to solve the situation. Since Spokend is a democracy all the citizens come to the meeting but their voices are ignored – especially the voice of one of the poorer citizens of the community suffering from a squeak that can only be cured with oil, Spare Wheel and his wife Fifth Wheel. Despite Spare Wheel's desperate pleas for oil, he is ignored and sent home without any help or consideration.

Without oil, Spare Wheel's squeak becomes so bad he loses his job and his family starts to suffer when his sick leave and unemployment benefits run out. What is he to do? Spare Wheel and Fifth Wheel develop a scheme that uses the squeak to their advantage against the town magistrate Big Wheel who finally relents and gives over the oil. Thus, for years after in the town of Spokend citizens in need of help are told "It's the squeaky wheel that gets the oil."

NOW AVAILABLE!!!

Broken Memories

Three teenagers come together with totally different lives and share their grievances through a collection of poems and stories of their life, because they feel that they have no voice in this world.

A passionate expression of the feelings, actions and reactions to issues that lodge themselves in the lives of three teens. An explosion of movement, music and story.

Made in the USA
San Bernardino, CA
17 June 2013